The Turning

Books by Ricardo Pau-Llosa

Sorting Metaphors
Bread of the Imagined
Cuba
Vereda Tropical
The Mastery Impulse
Parable Hunter
Man
The Turning

The Turning

Ricardo Pau-Llosa

Carnegie Mellon University Press
Pittsburgh 2018

Acknowledgments

Grateful acknowledgment is made to the magazines in which the poems in this collection first appeared:

The American Literary Review: "Artemis: View of Actaeon"; *The American Poetry Review*: "Ghost Orchid," "The Red Case"; *The Antigonish Review*: "Fan"; *Arion*: "Ariadne, Crete," "Daytime Moon," "Ogygia"; *Atlanta Review*: "Lagos de Covadonga"; *Barrow Street*: "The Prodigal's Brother"; *Bellevue Literary Review*: "Infanta"; *Beloit Poetry Journal*: "Dove Lake"; *Birmingham Poetry Review*: "Bruges," "Rings," "Sons-in-Law, Sodom," *"View of Toledo"*; *Boulevard*: "Wedding, Port-au-Prince"; *Caliban*: "Illuminations"; *The Cape Rock*: "A Byzantine Carving of Orpheus"; *Chariton Review*: "Artemisa Japanese Car Care, Miami"; *Christianity and Literature*: "The Elevator," "Papyrus Fragments"; *Cimarron Review*: "Siege"; *The Cincinnati Review*: "Phalaenopsis"; *Clackamas Literary Review*: "After Han Gan, Groom with Two Horses"; *CutBank*: "Flying above Missouri"; *The Dalhousie Review*: "Guillaume de Machaut: Arguments," "Variation on Quevedo's Variation on Seneca, Ovid"; *december*: "Little Ones," *"Popoloso deserto,"* "The Turning"; *Ekphrasis*: "Assyria at the British Museum" (winner of Ekphrasis Prize 2016); *Epoch*: *"The Menin Road (1918)," "Visteme despacio que voy de prisa," "Lupanar"*; *The Fiddlehead*: "Cerbatana, Yanomami," "Kensington," *"Tierra Adentro* (Inland)," "Regina"; *Harvard Review (online)*: "Luxury"; *Hiram Poetry Review*: "Actaeon, Closing Arguments"; *The Hollins Critic*: "At the Chest of Drawers (1936)"; *The Hudson Review*: "Reef"; *Island*: "Anno Domini 452"; *Kestrel*: "Idea of Order at the Metropolitan Museum," "En Plein Air"; *The Literary Review*: "Bath"; *MARGIE*: "Beggar," *"Cartoneros,* Buenos Aires"; *Mid-American Review*: "Farm"; *Natural Bridge*: "Plural"; *New England Review*: "Allegory of Art"; *Passages North*: "Eva Tropical," "Nkonda: Clearing a Path"; *Ploughshares*: "Summer, Florida Keys"; *Plume Poetry*: "GDR China," "Lamb," "Squandered Moons," *"Thetis,"* "Variation and Extension of 'Flower Shadows' by Su Shi (1037-1101)"; *PN Review*: "Clearing the Florida Coast," "Job 28:9-13"; *Post Road*: "Port of Miami, from the MacArthur Causeway"; *Reed*: "Indexical Reflection"; *River Styx*: "Castillon"; *Saranac Review*: "Delta," *"El Expolio,"* "Isabeau," "Narcissus"; *Saw Palm*: "Monsters"; *The Southern Review*: "Barbas," "Soldiers Washing (1927)"; *Southwest Review*: "Storm"; *Stand*: "Moon over Barcelona," "Rembrandt's Andromeda"; *32 Poems*: "Reflections at MMA Masters, Miami"; *Virginia Quarterly Review*: "Cuba, Where Art Thou?," "Husserlian Meditation," *"Solvitur Ambulando"*; *Volt*: "Democracy,"

Book design by Rissa Lee

Library of Congress Control Number 2018935065
ISBN 978-0-88748-639-5

in memory of Manolo Rodríguez, *mi padrino*

Even the dogs eat the crumbs that fall from their master's table.

—Matthew 15:27 (NIV)

So I have seen a river, where nothing obstructs its passage, flow calmly and with little noise, but rage and foam wherever trees and obstacles of stone held it back, fiercer for the obstruction.

—Ovid, *Metamorphoses* 3:571 (Kline tr.)

Contents

I.

II.

I.

Wedding, Port-au-Prince

after the painting by Wilson Bigaud

In the painting by Bigaud, a wall
has dropped to let us watch the feast
of drink and gossip. Strokes of guests
bubble up the window, as dancers scroll
the horizon of the painted living room.
The scene makes us hear the celebrant
trot and gaggle, and taste the scandent
mounds of food. Next door, the groom
and bride sit neatly on their bed,
and take refreshments from a gallant girl.
In this deaf scene, touch unfurls
the numb dress hung and the quilted spread.
At center stage, the jilted turns her face
to find a world within this broken place.

Eva Tropical

after the painting by Mario Carreño

We know Carreño dreamt the faceless nude—
one breast exposed, the other draped in hand—
though her poise be Ingres. She made her stand
outside the window with all of nature
at her back. Our view's been left inside,
framed by sill, making the pages of the scene
incongruous. She ought instead
to be the master of the room, serene
in shelter, and we, in eyes wrought wild,
the honed men the forest could not hold,
animated to take on the burden
of multiplicity. Who wouldn't
father guardianship and myriad duties
to be watched in love by a woman with no eyes?

Nkonda: Clearing a Path

after the painting by José Bedia

Bedia's man of thorns had earned each one,
as had the fragile shadow that he cast—
preserving the stick of figure and the bitter rungs.
His head, however, panned as a deer's. Fast
the man and himself had hoped to flee
from the woman's spirit, flowering on the lake,
calling out to them, "O, do not take,
that road, my dear!" for in it she could see
no purgation. But the stag only sought
silence, unable to halt Actaeon's hounds
nor in Aulis become the princess caught,
and instead was driven mad in the churning rounds.
Strange how her ripples part him from confusion
though he confuses this with absolution.

Barbas

after Titian's The Allegory of Age Governed by Prudence

The Spanish often say, *God gives*
beards to those who have no jaws,
to mean He plays dice or tenders clues,
hides his fumbles from the common view,
or quietly mocks what He will not cure.
Or makes of randomness the rule of laws
whose point and purpose we cannot receive
yet take for constancy. My girlfriend insists
it could also signify compensation,
For then—this woman without Spanish persists—
the beard would cover up the lack of chin,
and in the sway of life there'd be accounting
at the wheel. Jabber, jabber, I say to her,
no native to need, you are indeed a foreigner.

Thetis

after the painting Thetis (Aquarium) *by Robaldo Rodríguez*

We see her through her element, not
in it, a face of harvest and sand gazing
upon a crypt of waters, fish jotting
the tight firmament. The water bends
her to fill this pane and tints her face
into nature. She ignores these mere effects,
dragged inward by the pull of another tide,
welcoming the nobody she finds there at rest,
as a creature of bright scales finds respite
in crevices where her lights are blind.
Glints weave paths across the face and tank
to mark the painting's solitary and troubled link
to the instant, for a goddess needs no shield from time.
Her son, it's true, has cast his fate with might.

Rembrandt's Andromeda

Pride, too, whitens like a bone with fear,
swerves left as she gazes on the modern flat
grayness to our right for turmoil, signs that
the promised rage has come. No one hears
her last words, and there is no fighting
the punctual decree. At this point, the hero
soars invisibly and the lurking monster slows
beneath the waves, tired of roar and ravaging
the vain coast and wondering if it, too, is not
a prisoner of justice. Can a hunger he cannot sate
be drowned by this swallowed girl that hate
has cuffed to the polished, pumice, ashen rock?
The bronze leaves rustle. The snakes descend
upon the snake, freeing it, too, at tale's end.

But let us backtrack a bit, to the scene before us,
the girl pale as marble, no doubt the painter's
joke on goddesses stiff and cold. Any fainter
and she'd collapse bloodless as on a cross,
presaging a story the artist knows, so distant
is the teller from what is told. Ancients have it
the hero flew to stab the twisting serpent,
since monsters cannot die by a monster's habit.
He'll save the stone's ambition for the wedding fray
where a rival can indeed be turned to art.
Gratitude is the greater weapon of the cautious heart.
What angel bids her daily to look away
so an artless turn won't lock her in his granite
gallery? Strange gifts eternity has granted.

Dove Lake

after Thomas Eakins' Swimming *(1885)*

The figures mount, peak, and dive into stasis,
a frieze of youthful males in the raw that yet
reflect, as does a chain of words, a sentence's
urgent roll into a single thought.

Such is flesh, even the undesired,
that—brute as sun, untainted by veil—
it should lure the fervent eye from its tired
enclave. And yet, beauty will never fail

to riddle the mind, impugn the soft contrivance,
baffle instinct. The candid joys, in trance
with bodies on rock and font, close and dance

in verticals and pyramid, in measures,
that the compassing eye might guard the fissure—
dressed and healed—between scene and desire.

En Plein Air

A band of soldiers resting in a field is no
picnic—unless the war is won and the village
women are loitering. Wine. Clouds shaking
the brambles of gypsophila. Wine. Eating
is with hands, and sex half-clothed. Caged
fears are loosed. A farm barrels in shadow
beyond the nimbus of leaves trembling. A girl
emerges. A soldier. Crash in the distance rattles,
but then they settle into the summer of moment
again. Wine. The dust inhales. No lament
can disdain. Noon and Grain. No mantles
on the grass. The heat lenses in a whirl.
Away, a painter changes stratus to cumulus,
wheat to vines. A hill there, he'll lose.

Soldiers Washing (1927)

after the painting by Stanley Spencer

Even washing is a task, in war and daily
life. The warm and pour, the fresh linen,
the hourglass of soap in its melt telling
us how our tired flesh gleams to fiction
renewal. Time is at war. We are meant to lose
that we may grasp what we know: the waste
of passioned effort. The soldier nearest to us
dunks his face in the bowl, a murky foretaste
of baptismal death. This halo we discover
from which he'll surely rise, suspender cords
rhyming the sink. Next to him another
wrings the towel and turns his head toward
Bellona. Not incongruous. The patroness,
too, of the trench of days and the hearth's duress.

Reflections at MMA Masters, Miami

for my cousin Ricardo Lamas, "The Bully"

Were these not billed as martial *arts*, I might
resist the thresholds painting and ballet provide.
But memory, as muse, is identity's loyal dog,
and what Bellows forgot Balanchine recovers,
brings into focus, plants in the garden of immanence.

They roll and, with a plosive clap, the mat
rings with their flanks. The stone torsos ride
the wheel of blurs of their arms, each leg
gauzing sight. I see why Rilke started over
his life of the mind before speed's radiance,

however archaic the pretext. The fighters dance
to blows that mimic music's clock of gesture.
The arm arcs, the head sinks, all in the cog
and score of an exercise as the bodies jitter and glide.
They stop to think their suddenness, wrap tight

their wrists, and resume to bleed all chance
from the coming battle. For this they yearn to endure
the timeless sharpening, to promontory from the fog
of the quotidian and earn a victory that will not hide
in hope or prophesy. A fairer art, to fight.

Infanta

Meninas *(1656)*

Her glance, muse brittle, only starts
the tale of scene where paint and princess
interrupt each other. Velázquez
resumed the past and present and saw art's
future—the snapshot, Expressionism, identity
as ambiguity, the theatrical infinite, the irrelevance
of biography, impulse, and detail. As in the trance
in which the shaman dissolved dimensionality
itself, the painter is both observer and observed,
equal denizen of locked and brethren worlds.
Innocence is the playful infinite—the artist and child's
luxury. The king of copious faces is best served
in dim hover. As the only subject
of his world, he rules only what he reflects.

Moon over Barcelona

Rambla de Catalunya, 14 June '14

The way my balding father parted his hair
left a moon of skin to shimmer with toil.
He dreamt of walking these leafy ramblas
and never did. Labor's love affair,
exile's clockless plow, and launching children
precluded travels. The epic of the prismed life
he bequeathed to me, cigar in hand,
sliding down a boulevard rife
with fat tourists, a whore or two, nervy waiters,
and blurred youth skating to their thin doom.
In the tonsure between the branches, a full moon
erases fists of clouds the way a father's
memory restores the quiet to a path.
There is no first journey, only the last.

GDR China

My housekeeper had the dishes brought
from Cuba. Her husband then had swapped
jewelry for a color TV and East German plates.
Gold pattern inside the rim, and beneath it
a burgundy stripe. Their sturdy forms are boring
and the white all too white, the porcelain
not diaphanous. Their history, though,
embellishes them. Communism clinging
to its hated bourgeois persona. We too,
the clanging dishes say, can refine
the daily bread of unequal toil. Here, free,
she cleans houses, is richer and happy
to let these memories go. She calls them
the *balsero* service for six. Germany one, Cuba
disintegrating. What meals history serves up.

Tierra Adentro (Inland)

after the painting by José María Mijares

What was different in her from the women
Mijares conceived as *habaneras?* The maze
of ardent hair that conched into jewel and lace,
and braids, almost bones of silk, did garland
both his nacred dream of elegance
and this carnate woman, nude and flayed.
Risen from the earth against a drop of fleshed
forms, voluptuary in blues and greens,
that his older work quoted from stained-glass
traceries and the cubism of the dirty port.
Now the role of garment, stripped of splendor,
fell to a wrap of organs folding, stylized.
Her neck a flute, her head a triangle, for base
the square of arm and breast. Her face a contrabass.

Ghost Orchid

for Robert McKnight, after his sculptures

Haunted by the promise of flowers, light pursues
light, laps like water stolen to the salted
shore, pretends by sure bends the crafted
journey. It brings this brood of forms and hues

to us in twists that fiction the straight line
as the icon of truth. Veracity is of a different
mind—mantled, fluted, bone translucent
and smoke sprung from veined roots that vine

unleaved upon a trunk. It hovers seeming
in what fractions time allows to argue
the impossible beauty. The mute bewildered true
will not be ruler tamed nor taunt the reaping

of causalities. It will appear, vessel
glow, in rebel stillness, forbidden to settle.

Storm

after the painting by George Inness

The wind searches for a whiteness of its own,
and for that it shuffles trash, lugs the furniture
of clouds, fiddles with refractories,
to amass, from noon grays, the sudden tungsten

of a distant farmhouse, the steel of egrets
unhinged from uncombed branches. One has torn
itself from its failing trunk to claim the foreground
on the newly bristled green. We forget

the hidden lust things have for true
colors. How the withered leaves bronze
scalding in this untimed, gust-inflicted dawn's
theatric. Weather plows the tired blue.

We see the world through a tunnel's partial fist
or lose detail, starve and think it feast.

The Red Case

after Still Life #11, *a photograph by Cristian del Risco*

What nests things are, especially in the doze
of storage. On the closet shelf, a black purse
folded atop a bright red suitcase
and beside it a yellow box for one of those

old Brownie 500 Movie Projectors.
It is their color confluence which has caught
the need, exposed the weakness that is art.
The eye's edict of the scepter-lensed photographer

commands we look passionately outside ourselves
and coldly into ourselves, for every shelter
betrays its urgent walls. This is the better
part of native, nurturing nakedness.

What roosts in possession? Who will beckon it
to fly, find its kind, and prey upon it?

Any armoire, the most disheveled bin,
or the fittest regiment of ordered space
clusters infinites, demure privacies.
They city the many turgid hearths within

and likewise leave us vagrant, drizzled, shunned.
Let us say the projector is inside its box.
The home movies it ticked silent as a clock
hosted the feasts of a family long gone.

And even if we, insisting, took it out,
and pried the suitcase filled with old photos

of people whose far-thrown loves are also lost
in time, nothing can resist the rout

of memory an image crafts. The present kilns
the chance of beauty. The past can only burn.

And so we're left with volumes in this night
of the mind, and the gathering of red, yellow, and black
obscuring what hides inside them on this rack
beneath the languor of a glove's painful white.

It dangles in the foreground, propped or from a higher
shelf hung, tasseled, a groping moon
trapped like a frantic bird that burst into a room
and, stripped of nature, is the sudden exile

in alien epics and catalogs. It hopes for another's
darkness that it might point to blurs it knows.
For now, denied allegory, its role is to glow
in the enclosure and procure the snare of theater.

The hand will not come to it, but the eye will,
and the need, always, for what is beautiful.

Allegory of Art

for Yuyú

Unclear how my cousin has come to master hunger
in wild birds. They call him, or he them
by a quick whistle against his open palm
or the rattle of worms and corn the songbird

hears inside the plastic case. Often
they spy him deep among his orchids and stare
at him one eye at a time. However spare
their frames, he catches their presence, then

looks up to verify his favorite mockingbird
or the loggerhead shrike, or both. He makes me
sit quiet and still and tosses a worm to see
which one will feed in midair and which, unafraid,

would rather come to his fingertips and pluck
his morsels, that nearness alone should leave us
awestruck.

Bruges

Who can boast a fuller life than the artist,
a stranger feast of disparate plates,
one more replete even in emptiness?

The farmer clocks, by the merry of his harvest,
the lunar faces of his worth in crates.
Who can boast a fuller life than the artist?

Alone he births a beauty none can resist,
that cannot shape the clay of their earthly fates
yet makes them feel replete, even in emptiness.

The soldier, altaring life with sword, is the bravest
groom of glory with which alone he mates.
Who can boast a fuller life than the artist

whose labor, long after him, wins the truest
victories? His living work no funeral awaits.
Burns obscure, none more replete in emptiness.

Yet, to gather pearls from punishment he's cursed,
to magic loneliness, to mock happiness' estate.
Why does he boast a full life, this artist
who'd rather be replete than hoard emptiness?

Phalaenopsis

It hides its counterpoint of leaves, berets
that thicken from mossy nests in shades,
and weaves its gray snake roots around
the thin but sturdy trunks in darkness rationed
to harvest out the sun. When the time
comes to blossom, it neither clings nor climbs
but arcs a stem in search of patent brilliance
that it might pour forth the petulance
of its crop. Hung in tiers in bannered light,
solvent of the opaque, machine, home-tight
and dutiful, indebted to denial. Visible
only to the beauty-bored, the anchor of accolades
knows perfectly the wages of light are death,
so it balances shades to testify the feasible.

Plural

The octopus appears to be a viper's nest.
Forget the coded shades emotions taint
or the thoughtful eye that pries a problem loose
as when a sunken jar where prey's at rest
is unlid by the sleevy head that figures
the use of eight extremities when four would do.
There is comfort to so soft a beast
that signs its flight with ghosts of paint,
whose flesh a crack of rock will veil in hue.
Each arm will score the fold of its embrace
as if tide or fickleness controlled the crew,
and there were no center, no law, to tame
these forces into provinces.
A mane of coils makes art of dissidence.

Ariadne, Crete

It is natural to betray all one's known;
let no one damn what desire compasses.
As none can plot the knotted paths
of comets, neither can they ascertain
why the moon disfigures that part of itself
whose pumice proves it shrouds the truth.
The star-skilled may abacus our mother's
course, ignoring the reason she flees
in brilliant steps. Medea, too, disowned
a father and a land to heed her passion's call.
A bloody sun did free her, dragons, fire and all,
that she, like Helen, should always reign
and never render account of doomed decision.
Even regret is fated and glory bound to stain.

El Expolio

after Doménikos Theotokópoulos (El Greco), The Disrobing of Christ

The heads rubble together like bitter scraps
of once life moiled in a spring flood.
But it's the captive, dressed in his own blood,
who is dragged, bound. His eyes are the traps
of the spirit, his body and hand shepherd the lamb
of moment to the patient end. From mid-scene
an arm arches toward us, fingers accusing
the prisoner and, past him, us. What damns
the hostage is a mystery to the snarl of faces
churning the surface but locked bleak within
their private miniscules. Their growls and fists demand
precious little—a chance to get a few paces
from spectacle, some cloth. The convicted
one alone knows the reason he's rejected.

He is a foreigner, in land as in purpose.
A mad king, a kindling cradle, a dark hunger
brought him to this capital to fall under
suspicion for works the future holds virtuous.
And prophetic. The scene is flattened
by a tide of heads, and the red robe reveals
how a space chiseled into planes congeals
the paradox of the martyr with that of the orphaned
artist. How like an egg against the harsh
straw, a coin in the vaulting earth, a whisper
in the arena, they both must bring the world closer
the more it riles and hates in the luxury of its brash
ignorance. How moot light renders the present
with its store of silence, blood, and absence.

Isabeau

(c. 1370–1435), Queen consort of France, mother of Charles VII

I must have been insane or too young
to come here, be crowned, reign.
Even rule when love demanded I rein
in the state. The king could not function.
Wolves of dukes, France a brittle mess.
No one cared if even then I longed for home
and peace, but I tied the sails to the frantic mast,
for a son and honor's sake. Duty's done
when the self's betrayed. More Odysseus
than Penelope, I heard the song in the storm
and claimed my residence there, in blows reborn,
that this my land, I, the proud judicious
foreign queen, might balance back to health.
On the fleur-de-lis, no petal marks the self.

Castillon

1453

A field of moans and the dead is paradise
when, at last, it is the enemy that feeds
the crows and dogs. In early victories
they grinned bemused at our strewn lords,
pried their armor loose, hacked for rings,
trophied thick their halls with our defeat.
Causeless, they could loot, boast, and sing,
but they could never, in just death, delight
in a debt repaid, soul for soul. Ours
is the heaven of the balanced scales. The heart's munition
of lament is on this day the trumpeter
that closes one epic that another may open.
Our manna, their dead. We are a nation forever
free to chore remembrance in quiet honor.

Guillaume de Machaut: Arguments

poet, composer (1300–1377)

-1-

Those who wrecked then saved dear France
are not the same, and are the same, two notes
I will marry to a syllable stretching for order.
Voice is not the field but the wanderer
who, filled, must fill with life both stern motets
and ardor's virelais. What chords don't dance?
But art cannot repair a broken land,
nor can balms cure, nor pain subside
by searing vision's cue or music's ponder.
These words in poems may charm the lute,
but they must journey into laws before
they can shape and not just praise life.
And brave and commoner, miter and crown alike
must find in Justice paradise, and ask no more.

-2-

Until that day comes, let us
endure with art what art cannot cure.
Let us stain the paltry glass with lapis
and carnelian—make beauty life's decree
and punish ugliness, savagery, and sloth
with forced immersion in the font of poetry.
Let not the moneyed brute say he ought
to tend his lands, defend his property,
nor let the sworded drunk confuse his revelry
with the dutiful joys. Ideas have their ribaldry,
and loose within the harem's heart, they engineer
what otherwise would flood. Hence, beauty wrought
merits time and instinct. Art's empire
scoffs, imperils, gorges—even at times inspires.

Narcissus

When the young come to know themselves, they kill
the love once felt for yearning and desire.
Not the pangs themselves, but the cult of fire
beside the placid pond whose moons fill
with thrown light. They slaughter the ante-feeling
and the afterthought together, leaving themselves
as they might a tip or a splintered cry who loves
them still too much. In truth, they're reeling
from an unframed view which duty beckons
them to embrace—a world and them without
a hint of measure, nowhere a splat or jot
of directive where once, with the pearled bone
of shallow rays, a moon did spill the night,
upstaging darkness, callous bright.

Lagos de Covadonga

Asturias, Spain

No quiet desperation here, only the swell
of mountain winds, the clang of a cowbell
and rumored weather. A few visitors snap
pictures of the ochre cattle with a snowy cap
and the tongue of mercurial lake as backdrop.
A dragonfly, awkward in this reedless crop
of low grass, jabs and halts the air
like the rhythm with which a writer's hand snares
thought. This race for pauses and some light
ignores the tourist, the innkeeper, and the guide,
all the infantry in a life without generals.
They huddle in the particulars of the grimy, feral
moment. Appetite pulling rank over cause.
History is their swallowed song from a passing hearse.

The Turning

for José Rodríguez–Dod

An early commission plants roundhouse and train
in Inness' *Lackawanna Valley.* The Railroad wants
its due as Scranton and America flex their brawn.
As nature fuzzes, we ask, Who's the respondent
and who the lead singer in the scene, the engine
or the reclining youth in straw hat and red vest,
disputing center stage with the dark machine?
A platoon of haystacks blur but gather as best
they can against the ardent green, for the enemy
approaches on a scythe of tracks and will not tarry
to face defeat or claim an obvious victory.
The train has somewhere to get to and time
is money. The artist turned away from man's
rumblings after this, to cloud the lands

he saw with spirit. A sower of balances, Inness
would often paint a lone human in a landscape
buzzed with a cottony glaze, a dreamy drape
of blues and earths. The sentinel in the canvas
convinces us that what and how he witnesses
is our view as well, a nebula we can't escape.
These mists of birth cradle the molten cypress
and the gelling fog, the mountain's languid nape
and the basket of all consciousness: the lake
or sea, the river or the vapor from the train.
Water is the signature in the solemn contract
between light and matter. The figure is the refrain
in a siren's monologue sung upon a vapid stage
of naturals, that celebrates the loneliness of the age.

Variation and Extension of "Flower Shadows" by Su Shi (1037-1101)

By day, the marble terrace piles their vagrant grays.
That dozing servant of mine fails to sweep them away.

What point to wait for the setting sun to do your job?
The bright moon plots their return, you lazy boy.

The flickering shadows will always linger, you say indignant.
You think me dense, do you? In vain I proffer the poignant

lesson. I who have wandered in the company of my thoughts,
who once told regions how to live and float

on rivers I had bent and dug, on bridges I
had spun and arced. I who made numbers sigh

to words, and words in strokes respond to angled lights.
I've swept the paths I made with clogs by rain and night,

not with brooms but with my steps, that shadows lose
their tribe and call when stumbling upon my tracks confused.

By addition I remove, by semblance populate
my time, that unserved I dare this troubled way.

The Elevator

One grows into the grate of arrival, the jarring
scrape of steel tiring railings into unknown
moans at once mechanical and bestiary,
where a voice almost seeks the seed of human
grumbling. Surely it is the daily mount
that marks the comfort, then the trope, then
the need for the now scripted friction to open
the door 2.6 seconds after the last sound
which startles only those who've never risen
this course, to this floor, in this building
and turning, raft upon my unshaken boredom
their urgent need for shelter in the function
of this cracking world, this egg, a clock
that textures time by groans and jolts in a box.

Papyrus Fragments

They move, these bitten isles, between voids
time has scribed. Here lie two tales at once.
One in shards, like wings between two panes,
lessons love. This frail colony of words

fills the gaps with suppositions, contriving
dim stars and dark matter from the lights
we do see. Behold how among bright
peaks we loiter lines, with shapes divining

the monster and its hero, the maiden's curse
and the son's return. We cannot bear
to leave alone the erasures mind abhors,
but in those tides the silent truths rehearse

our intimate closure. Beware the ark of dream.
Image stars alone, unpaired by word or scheme.

Squandered Moons

Probes on TV tell the tale of their
worthlessness—all rock and frozen acid,
enough ammonia to shine the pane of a solar
system. Beneath an ice cap's green and limpid
tide, the bets are off on whether cell-bright
creatures stir which breathe that leaden wash.
No more austere than our lone satellite,
their deck of molts is etched in the crack and splash
of wombed volcanoes clocked in gelid rage.
It is not chaos that herds them away from us,
but the laws of dearth whose iron, wealth, and range
edict the plenitude of shackled stillness.
Behold the spirit of our stubborn nature there,
the rocky proud before the destitute mirror.

Rings

Distance gels the ghostly into fictions
of solidity. Dust and wrecked ice
shimmer in bands of alternating light
and dark, pretending the disk-tight spins.
Nothing perspective cannot counterfeit.
Giant planets that pull the reins of space
are but rounded clouds, hardly fit
by logic to pluck a harp. Their surfaces race
centuries of storms, one wide enough to gulp
an earth in its crimson eye. As saintly painters
halo beings of the light, the culpable
laurel tinsel on whirls of worldly raptures.
There is no intimate mirage—nearness knows.
Ask the mournful, when their hour is close.

View of Toledo

after the painting by Doménikos Theotokópoulos (El Greco),
for Candelas Gala

The cobalt tempest has turned the gravestone grays
into rubbed silver. The scalding greens spill
onto the river of viewpoint, defying size,
untrusting sense. Blinks of Tajo fulfill

the painter's ramparts in the real, though spires shift
and bushes cypress into flame, and the mind lifts
only to perch on the ancient city of new men.
But for a moment, reality is the miracle where human

stone and land have first mated beneath
a marble storm. The prayer antiquities wreath
generations into folding rings of need, a chess
whose moves we've come to know as kingless.

Triumph here but do not beg for light,
or fray with vision and scorn the world's sure night.

Delta

The poisoned sea turns to peanut butter
from the plane window, a rimless jar whose plain
vastness jolts me back to the book lying
on my lap. Smoking is forbidden but not the murder
of a coast from whose sundry depths an armada
of jellies, like bodiless gills, gasp risen
into folding shallows. Caring little for the barren
nature of this soup, their strands reach farther
to bristle with arthropods, lone morsels in a harem
of hunger. Blind, they make of turbid waters
their garden. Their flapping bells with many clappers
mock the ear as well. The dank requiem
is a madrigal to the opal species who masters
artfully the rudiments of life's pendulum.

Husserlian Meditation

The squirrels deny themselves from front and back
and only word into view from the sides when
their outline rejects the coup of geometry.
From the south we delight in the polar symmetry
of their foggy tails cupped by rounded hinds.
North, the nutshell of head lacks
an easy grasp. East is west for us,
their weight by buried muscles held
so that the tail and torso deceive in balance.
What made them thus is unstudied grace
which I unmake and recompose, compelled
to translate experience into coded fuss.
The beast will feed and leave the watchers to maze
their habits and splice contortions into ballets.

Reef

The cameras save us from drowning or becoming
a meal as they borrow our eyes to conceive a world
whose strangeness we've come to need. Swayed rock
that nibbles and mates, claws and coils whirling
to hunger's tune. Beauty is Andromeda's work,

chained to taut patience whose only promise
is a dawning grumble. Blessed are the colorful
for they are poisonous. Blessed the dark
for they have learned to count. Blessed the callous
who have armored virtue. Blessed the crafty

for they learn alone. Blessed the camouflaged
for only they know themselves. Blessed
are the bioluminescent for they rhythm
emptiness. Blessed the innumerable besieged
for their fear feeds throngs. Blessed the brimming

pools which turn the ocean into a word.
Standing over them we lock reduction
into our view of the self. Contained, the held
bright myriad whose torments clear and urchins
jewel, rise unbroken and unshelled.

Farm

after the painting by Piki Mendizabal

Florida is the horizon defeated by fences.
Over the hedge, thatch roofs pretend hills
while a gauze of grasses splits the path
toward distance into two rails of rocky flesh.
A worker leans over decoratives in black pails

which regiment the field. Blessed are the fruitless which forest
the mind with tropes. Blessed the insects for whom
poison seasons a meal. Blessed the toolmaker
who signs the earth in absentia. Blessed the mole
whose city is dark, urgent, and mute. Blessed the owl

whose hunger feeds the true children of the house.
Blessed is the surveyor who pacifies with numbers, and the
digger of cisterns—the moralist of ruin and of plenty. Blessed
is the planter who writes the story seeds will disown.
The cult of openness makes the eye digress

past eight posts, four on each side,
of the path foreground. On the right
a red shirt jolts and complements.
Toil's flag is the field itself, factory straight.
The shirt, however, rules the field in our mind.

Artemis: View of Actaeon

Had he lingered in his gaze he might have stayed
a man for the luring would have blessed him, that doggèd
stare through leaves upon the sudden feast.
Later the story, to save him, has him the beast
whose nature turned him, whose animals could not
help him beyond themselves. No beauty brought
him to the wilds with rancorous bow, the flight
of prey crisping nostril and pupil, rousing the might
of skill against nature's odds. Perhaps as a boy
almost still, fumbling with shaft and decoy,
he strayed suffused before pure beauty
in a virile guise, and he recoiled, in duty
as a new man. This led him to renounce
all harmonies and graces lest they announce
again the dread enchantment with one's own.
I've seen them prowling in my verdant zone,
strapping branches to their heads and backs,
studying the frailest echo of lusted tracks,
and burying themselves in the chore to kill
antler, tusk, and hide which, in truth, fulfill
the role of what they cannot undo in the mind.
Who could otherwise neglect woman's kind
in art, food, music, in the sway of cloud
or the pages of a brook, even in the hound
at rest, lustrous if impatient, even in gold?
In nothing do they find the petal's damp fold
or the harp's embrace, for a shadow of their sex
has possessed and eclipsed any and all objects
of desire, born as this must always be
from aesthetic appetite. Poorest, never free,
the hunter lost in weapon and image hunts

himself, despising what he cannot confront,
abjuring the happiness of those caught
up in the porcelain wine and silken plot
where woman and her art take their place
as the goal and prayer of every chase.

II.

A Byzantine Carving of Orpheus

He strums his lyre in stone
in Greek to hover on salvation's dome
and leave his classical womb behind.

The animals in awe halo music's prince,
as they never did with Noah, cramped
in his dark duty, waiting to be free

to ignore the soldier's steadfast
and take the hills, the plains again,
breed and kill each other, resume

the melody of a bloody life, the only
one they've been allowed to know.
Orpheus tried to tame the common beast

and the triple dog, the god of death
and the dead girl. But he cannot leash
the irate mob who, snubbed, detest

loyalty and song. Who is he to grieve
while we yearn? Who is he who undoes
briefly death but will not calm such hearts?

Illuminations

at the British Library

Faith regardless,
gold frogs entwine
the pearl and blood sky,

reminding us who bend
over the fingerprint–mazed
glass, caught in the ambers

of learnèd halogens,
how in war newsreels
the lace of once cities

roiled in jumpy silence,
tongues turning
into Dresden

where the next books
were copied by priest
and rabbi who knew celestials

differently, so I shake
from mind the bleak
similitude pond

in which forms leap
into misnames,
with the help of a label

that assures this aureate
knit is no modern
thing but a letter

from a winged time;
ergo I saunter pensive
hands braided behind me

              in the scrubbed dark
      to the next case
where initial traceries

will again curdle
      clockless angels
            into radiator grills,

if the poem of present
will have it so.

Assyria at the British Museum

Lion hunt, *Palace of Ashurbanipal, Nineveh*

They never lacked for grace, the hunters
or the hunted, dancers of aim and lunge.

Or was this the effect of art exhaling
in jasmine strokes the tale of how

flesh kills in fear of its own allotment?
Decorous murals line the vanilla walls.

Down the paved river, heads flotsam,
halt, then flow again, draining

into the Greek galleries or Rome.
Uniforms litter the griffin gate.

Quick cameras hoard the lioness
anchoring her cry, aiming it at the sky

while her loins banner the dirt. Chariots
roll their muscled cargo of taut strings.

The calm of visitors prays these blanket
slaughters belong to sage and chronicle,

and that what hungers into our calendar
is pure skill, the slabs crystaled

by how art's surgeries have witnessed
such naked blood. Each life

worships on a bank—the hunter's
or the prey. Yet the current forbids

equally—who don pelts in formation
or fight perishing into stone.

The Menin Road (1918)

after the painting by Paul Nash

It is never early or late in war, for the howl of present
disowns time. Only later, in memory, do flesh
and rock mingle on a palette's harem, honey up
the crater silver with dank and drip, and otherwise

fight the treacherous battle of images against
death. How rhythm-perfect the stripped trunks
of guilty trees align, a ruptured cage
from which the throated birds beamed forth

into a patient sky. The soldiers scurry, fogging
our sense of whether they are the first or last
of an offensive offensive. In field, though not in art,
they must have trembled like medals or the missing

foliage which now the curve of metal and the shock
of crumpled rock must replace in the mind, for vacuums
bloom with novel candidates for twig and home.
The vines have been recalled by cuneiforms

of ditches in the distance, forbidding language a place
in no man's tongue. The colors chime; the blocks fall
like Cubist flanks of nude idea. Sky and land
search each other for purpose, cagey as beams.

Anno Domini 452

It is not the fish, their fate inscribed
in glass, nor the shrill of lights on scales
that draw us to the aquarium in Stanley Spencer's
Boatbuilder's Yard, Cookham (1936).
Two goldfish crypted, staring
out next to a stone that cannot
hide them. It's been left on the tiled patio
before a brick garden wall
and desert succulents among rocks
propped like polite rubble: coral
and travertine chunks anthologizing
shells and detritus that annotate
the gladly if unwisely forgotten. Beyond,
like flotsam petals, boats mire
the bank of a river sure to hold
its tongue through the coming war.
Beasts, we are told, presage calamity,
and so these fish might dream
their dim parcel a palace. Legend
has Attila, siege tired, reading
victory in the sudden flight of storks
from Aquileia. Its refugees
would found Venice. The fish
burn against the gravel gray
like flares above a trench.
All is alien to us in the tank,
except that brethren ground.
It is the bottom of the sea which makes it ours.

Kensington

The early joggers
like threadless needles
stab the monogram
car lights have etched.
They caution their race
yet cross the reeded
banks like a sure wind.
Versus the runners
on the north curve
of lunchtime Thames
about the obelisk.
They sear through
flocks of mappy tourists
indifferent
as the bronze
Victorian
sphinxes that bookend
Egypt. Beneath
one's chin
sits a Jamaican
doing business
on a cell phone,
sure yet remote
in his game,
eyes darting
to read figures
skyward or
in the wake
of a tour boat
named Sarpedon.
I sit on a bench
scribbling and smoking
a cigar while the Ferris wheel

dials its petulant eggs.
To the right
the masts of Hungerford's
walkway spider
a slow train,
proving we see movement first,
then its author,
as the tyger
was a tree-caged flame
before God's
golden remorse.
More river joggers,
and later walking
off dinner
near my hotel
about the park,
another troop
of racers bent
on keeping in shape
blur through
cabs and buses
rooted in afternoon
rush hour,
torches of sweaty hair
refusing for now to fade,
like letters in manuscripts
centuries have punished
yet still dance
about the void,
drunk on survival,
filling in the tatters
with their nervous
syntax of guesses.

Bath

Save the luxury of flicks
or a commercial
in which a siren
scales with suds
to sell beer, we are alien
to bathing as spectacle.

Gone are the Venuses
staged in white globules
of linen, a putto angling
a mirror, toiletted in air
and drying oils.
Their open stares
question our buttoned caves.

Or this liquid proscenium
where ancients
cool to unfurl,
got talky in the limpid
and, elbowed into busy flesh,
splashed thoughtless
as numbers in a ledger.

Now the vaults
and leaden pools
of dank aquaria
host tickets and cameras
coursing the clothed and somber
curious, recreating
with an audio guide's help
the marble animal casual
of these origins.

The roamers
stop dutifully
at a numbered cue
to study a capital's
blurred nymph,
then float on, absorbing
the stony wreck of erstwhile
brisk loin and cackle.
In history's tireless farm
the plough and the soil
cannot forgive each other.

Vísteme despacio que voy de prisa

Dress me slowly; I'm in a hurry.
—Spanish saying

Precipitation
attires the earth
in season and flood,
thumbs calendars,
scolds patience. Satiates
only to prepare the parched
chronicle. Unquestioned, it rages
like the hallowed free.
No fever of world lacks it—
volcano's mud, tornado's hail,
the quake that shrugs a sea upon us.
When it rules the mindless moment
in blizzard and hurricane, we grasp it
as the soul machinery of the soul-less.
Tinkling in our drinks, splashing the shower
or ranging the tossed boulders of clouds,
it co-signs the agreement
that all that gulps must drown.
Do not, then, fret on other symbols
of our promised detraction
in moths that twice alight
on the same shoulder, goblins doubling,
or shadows barking at the covered moon.
We, unnymphed but most aqueous,
know it's only natural to course
the field yet dry to hold us,
the sky punctual with clear fall,
the vessel hollowed with dusty music.
We dress the world—it will wait.

Job 28:9–13

for Lew Wilson

From bank or airplane rivers glitter
like stolen gems or blind like regret.

They ignite the prosperous
garden at night, luring trunks

and vines into their kinship. Throngs
of flows are disclosed by the same brilliance

that hammers stars our way; it courses
the hollows—a burin across dark matter.

Into gullies of light have planets
and poems rolled since brittle antiquity

to end with the shooting points
of a screensaver whose 3-D wheel

is axled by nothingness.
Any bled trickle, any branch

of water from a rinsed car or spilled drink
inking across pavement may well

darken its path across the hot world,
but like dove and lightning it is filled

with a light it can no longer hold.
Every question is a river, a sword

suddenly sprung from the laps of plumes
of the angel's bitter wings.

He plowed the moat that sundered paradise.
Its embers gild every river.

Clearing the Florida Coast

A gauze of blue tiles—contradictions at 8 a.m.,
the harvest of ascent. A quiet sea broken

by two white troughs, yacht calligraphies.
A horizoned stare thickens the air

into a white arctic depth hovering
over the soon Bahamas. Climbing still,

the plain illusions pull away like worn bandages.
Having dozed a watch-confirmed four minutes,

my eyes now settle on a smaller vaster sea,
pudding skinned. What dreams make boil

no stirring will calm. *Nata* in Spanish, the creamy
shell of boiled milk. Born indeed. Culled cells,

like all the quick, are urgent to claim breath.
Embryo is raised by the weight masonry

of living, that lurch to creature that drives
singulars into complex fora—anatomies, herds.

Behold lizard, moon and continent—chapters
in the fever gatherings. And we here sleeved

in the cabin, grains in the arrow's shaft fired
through the pool of the real, bubbling thoughts.

Summer, Florida Keys

Count on the storm to steel the waves,
tin their shimmer and heave. The electric
cracks sheen the air, particle its vapors,
and the wind that's coming has already
moved the sea, miles off. Shoreside,
we sense the sea has breathed in and readies.
Now, oiled by the hovering cobalt,
it simply rolls within itself like grain
in a sack a pair of fists is about to take
from dock to hold. Will throw the sack
on his shoulder, sweat will varnish his back,
and muscles will shift his flesh while the grain
finds its hourglass rules in the burlap dark.
We know the world's been held aloft
in punishment, and drowned in punishment.
But who carries it and why, to make of waves
a granary, of turquoise mirror a shroud?

Luxury

Biltmore Hotel, Coral Gables

It rose from mangrove, past canopy, screeches
of parrots hailing the clouds. Nothing human
but it for thirty miles or more.

Even then, only kin extravagances
tucked into savage coves: Deering's Vizcaya
Palace by the sea or the nervous caramel

of the Miami News tower. No city yet
made real by drudgery and fear. A haggard dock,
its amblers free with smuggled rum.

No law but pleasure in the wilds. Inland,
surrounding the creamy Biltmore's panic of styles—
Spanish Neoclassical Baroque Renaissance—

gondolas sprung along canals that snaked
between polo fields and golf courses.
The mounted rich hounded for foxes.

A small train chugged guests from the port
to our jazzy opera in the jungle. As it pulled city
toward its hems, it peopled forest

and drank the marsh, becoming a historical anomaly
instead of a human apparition in nature. Then
the Biltmore died for the first time.

Hushed, its foxes volleyed and mated in the moil
of suburban yards. The gondolas retreated into photographs,
as did the eleganti in nacreous breezes

and minty sips. War mended soldiers,
and peace drew a sheet over its face
for decades. When it flared its old

self—stucco flesh reswirled, velvets
reappointed—it could not pretend
that the huddled vanities of youth lingered.

The shepherd of a spirit's age can now beacon
the files we call tradition for those who can
afford to live without memory.

The Gables foxes lounge around birdbaths,
steal the cat food in a lonely bowl, and otherwise
thug the gardens from opossum and raccoon.

They glance an airplane seeming set in the full
dish of moon, red blinking lights
jewelling the utensils of the tower's antennae.

Popoloso deserto

La Traviata

The moon scorns this brittle town,
masked busy, airy, bubbling lights.
It knows itself known. It cannot
pretend a loss of face. Unredeemable
by duel or duet. It yawns
at this patch of roofs, pools,
and terraces, barking shutters
against the knife of night,
filled with the lunatic kind.

There are no songs about Miami,
save one quite old about her rival
who juts into scene, flutters
between the pages of broken gardens.
You'd think by now the gondolieri
would have seized the torch
of slow islands where exiles
taught the revenues of siege to glow.

Shine, instead. Atwitter
with a melt of trafficked lights,
confusion denies city. Not even
the great whore deigns to reign here.
There is no meander, no delicious stray
in her gait beneath the hemispheres
of her gown. Vibrato is not shudder.
It is ambition grown merry into voice.
No one here has heard such anthems.

So when the young man comes
to kill his heart for love, he must

slouch toward alleys behind clubs,
anchored by fake chains, ass
exposed. He becomes the dregs
he drags into himself, amnesiac,
unable to altar his future
on a rock with no lamb in sight.
No sense of time means
no pleasure, hence no path,
hence no divine perdition.

Port of Miami, from the MacArthur Causeway

It is the sea that is misplaced—
nervous bulk a cupped palm
can sweep into a glitter of dust.
On it the heaviest angles of rust
rise, laden. The hidden helm
lurks its screens and satellites

past rigging and chain, the ancient
mask of a familiar mystery.
Buoyancy is number's boring miracle,
the fruit of tangled sums and symbols
Greek with decimals. Would infinity
be as uncapped, we'd put a dent

in useless chatter about divine
conditions. The barge passes liners
loading cities of fat tourists
with boarding drinks in hand. The dizziest
outshout the tugging machinery
that likewise baffles the eye's supine

reasoning. In the Cave, even light
is shadow that mauls as it apes its origins.
Laws we must dive for. All else is ripple
and spray. A tipsy Cleopatra, visible
from here, points in spills to the towering
barge fading out of sight.

Flying above Missouri

Isaiah 5:13

By bends the river
weighs the ground's merit.
Angling
for a destined south
that now slopes
the other cardinals
to wherever
the dryness tows
calligraphy.

Internal shore,
the mind's pole
for the pumice flat,
it confounds
its predicate role.
The River is the verb
of the verb nation.

Lost it never seems
through arcs that will not
guide the geese chevron
or this plane
mapped and scheduled
between earth and heaven
gulping clouds in rows,
climate's abacus.

A chatty native in the next seat
pulls me to his boyhood "There."
These molten lights
breathed his dense, intended flow.

He's counted all his man days
since this water was his home.

Cradle, speaker, mast
upon which a people
swayed storm into course.
Briefly, as he rambles, I ponder
the landscape as would be mine.
I am fluent yet foreign
to its syllables.
Sibilant formed,
the spinal undulant
shapes the compass
by which a race I know
but will not know me
knows and is known.

After Han Gan, *Groom with Two Horses*

The man behind the blinds watches
the blackbirds eat the bread
and seeds he has scattered richly
on the concrete slab in his yard.

He ponders, the way the bellied groom
in the T'ang painting looks
at neither the white horse he sits on
nor the black one in the foreground which crooks

its head away from us. It leaves an outline
of the muzzle where the painter
figured his stallion would be by now.
Given there is no math to such turn

and jolt as beasts are prone to, and given
the painter projects himself into his work
as the groom, he inverts the yin
of outline and the yang of volume's dark

so, much as the man with his birds,
the painter can also capture gaze
and what he grasps at once. Thus he herds
together the many horses that graze

in the mind and the many who lose
color to become pure form, flat
yet full and moving. Studied rupture, like those
birds, hungry. Dabs against the matte

wet gray that blurs crumbs and presses
leaves into pleats of tunic. The groom's beard
is a coal smudge. In the sudden flight of the present—
the stallion's tail and doves, the dew and the bread.

Indexical Reflection

thinking of Charles Sanders Peirce

The blazer elbows confess,
thinning into the lightest shimmer,
the new silk old wools become.

Truly our robes know us.
Not merely because they buckle
into our shape. We are, indeed, the acrid

substance a spun air stands in for
in closets and bins. And we are the hope
of the soft shells dozing in dropped piles

on chairs, on bedroom floors. No poem
tells us better, no signature or print
reveals more. The bellied shirt,

the sock that holds the vault of foot
like a party's sighed balloon,
the cylindrical canvas of sleeve and leg,

and the stretched thread of a neck-fat button
will tabernacle a body, so no one need
betray himself. Alone among our possessions,

our clothes age faster than we do.
Gladly they ground themselves
on the reef of fashion, bid us to go on,

live, wear others out. Even as they lump
in bins—abandon's dark planets—they hum us
faithfully, like dogs, happy and bitter.

Cerbatana, Yanomami

Estado Bolívar, Venezuela

The blowgun is made of palm wood, for its hardness
and not its beauty. Although it cannot deny itself

aesthetic luxury, it is a weapon. The longer, the better.
The narrower, too. The darts, arrow length

and feathered, are tipped in poisons boiled
from plants, curare among others. The mouthpiece

is bone, and the hunter cups one hand around
his lips while pointing the *cerbatana* at prey

or enemy with the other. The beam that fathers
a beam, it trains mouth, arms, and lungs to ape

the eye whose aim never fails. How strange,
yet how inevitable, that the quiet eye,

the unthinking gaze of reflex and contemplation
wherein all marvels bulk as in a rich basket

carried over one's head across a river churning
with rock and life, how brazen and ineluctable

that we should hope to kill as naturally
as the eye finds, takes, and disowns the world.

Ogygia

after the painting A Fantastic Cave with Odysseus
and Calypso *by Jan Brueghel the Elder and Hendrick de
Clerck (1616)*

His best seven years I had, I took.
He didn't fight, ensconced in my dense
cave, riotous with perfumed fires,
fountains toppling onto each other
like memories squandered
in a harem of memories.

The silver of the place, its hammered
light, tripped from vines and the drench
of fruit. Nearby, diligent girls attended
so all we had to do was melt and sway.
He cups my breast while I sit on his lap,
as if he were the possessor.

The birds worked the sea
which leaked into view now and then,
harrying the fish and each other,
ungrateful their lives, however sung,
required daily toil. But they, after all,
are not the artists of any soul.
At best, servants of indifferent
transcendence. For him, I knew,
glory and family were rewards
greater than the gold in which
we ambered our pleasures.

Orders came, and I obeyed.
But I was the loser, in the end.
Mortal, he would sail to troubled home

and sometime die. This, our brevity,
would inflame his stubborn sail
with remembrance. I, endless,
must weave and unweave
the breaths I seized
into a coverlet for shivering infinity.

Idea of Order at The Metropolitan Museum

after Johannes Vermeer's A Young Woman Asleep

The man and the woman who met online
decided to meet at the museum,

to sublime in sync, a good start.
But she lied on the form about loving

beauty that never dies, and was bored—
overly eye-opened bored, performing

happiness as per body-language
cues from a magazine. The man, too,

though in his element, was bored,
having lied as well about how wide

his tastes ranged: art, stocks, arm wrestling,
jazz, of course, with a touch of punk now and then.

Look, he said, pointing to the Vermeer.
The woman mistook this for a challenge.

The girl in the painting slumps in a doze,
doubling in her dream the world we know,

but the woman now felt exposed,
the proscenium of her tedium breached.

The man lost himself, again, in patterns
woven into folds and clumps,

as if the blanket was still stored
in a careful trunk and the dreaming girl

had let us down into it with cords
her sleep trammeled by accident.

Propped yet no less lost to sleep,
the girl is dressed in wines that whisper

leather chair and tablecloths.
It is a shore the girl configures

on the table before her,
where the man and the woman meet

for the first time, in sandy nakedness,
and the glassy bonnets of jellyfish

fail across the frontal lobe of the sea
where hardness and algae push

the beery lip away and back.
The man notices the woman needs

caffeine or potassium, so up he had gotten
on nutrition and its yank upon the flesh.

Enough Vermeer, he said. She sighed
for nourishment. Still haunted

by the girl, the man asked his date
if she had noticed how, in the painting,

the wave of one intent
abandons the choral shapes

of fruit, wing and heraldry
rhythmed in loom. Not in these words,

exactly, but he felt the need
to know just how deeply it went for her,

the sleeping girl, the wafting shapes?
Isn't it clear, he would have loved to hear,

that the girl seeks in dream
the gift of being known at a glance,

unlike the waves we simply see as waves,
forbidding difference that they may rush,

cleanse, and extinguish in sibilants and thuds.
But that is not what he heard.

They would quibble, after coffee and cake,
over the check, the woman insisting on paying

half, and he countering it was his idea to meet,
but they went dutch, and that was the end of it.

Fan

He didn't really like the music of X,
but told his girlfriend, who was hearing
a borrowed CD, that he did, trying to be polite,
Really like that song playing now, he said,
and she went out and bought him the CD,
and he thanked her of course but later wished
he hadn't when, four months after they had broken up,
she came by with two more CDs for his birthday,
including the latest by X nominated for a Grammy,
and he felt now committed to the courtesy
of admiring X to her face although aching to just tell her,
X sucks harder than a black hole, rather than laugh
at her silliness in the mute calm of his burnt throat,
so he went on with Love it, Love it, and when she finally
faded out, some new woman came over
and saw all the X CDs and figured
he was the biggest fan, and he thought to himself,
O no, now I can't just dump on the music of X
because this new woman who's great in bed
will think I'm a nut having all of X's recordings
and loathing them, so she went and bought him more
CDs and told everyone they knew what a connoisseur
he was of X, that he had even met X, that X was a friend,
and he said No, not really, not at all, what she means is . . .
but to no avail, the CDs kept piling and the stories
grew until that woman was out and the new one and the one
after that one were simply told right off that indeed
he adored X's music, Live to hear it, we're best friends,
even helped X compose some of those songs,
because that seemed to make his life and CD collection
make enough sense for them to have sex with him

fairly quickly, and that kept going until one day
X sent him a card, which stunned him
because he wasn't in the music industry
or anything remotely like it, so why would famous X
write to him?, well because the stories had gotten back
that he had turned his entire life, his house, his car, his garage,
his underwear drawer into an X shrine and X was touched
and wanted his publicity guys to come over and take pictures
and maybe use them on an album cover or shoot a video
there, You know, X said, and he did, but his house
wasn't really a shrine until he noticed that the posters
and the pictures and the dolls had piled up
alongside the CDs, and, well, maybe it was
a shrine, and he was so flattered that X himself
had actually written the note and more so when X
followed up with a personal call, which really knocked him out,
so that when they shot the video some weeks later
and featured him as the ultimate X fan, he had no choice
but have a nervous breakdown and think about jumping
into Biscayne Bay when they discovered X in a cheap motel,
shot up with drugs naked next to the corpse
of the ex-girlfriend who had bought him his first X CD,
which made him realize that it was all a shrine to her,
to her of all people, To Her, he said beating himself up
between sobs and spit, a shrine to a middle-aged
druggie flatlined next to the worst singer who ever lived
and whom, he just knew, she had gotten tangled up
with because this was her way to live in the groove
of a love he couldn't return like borrowed tunes,
stuck and turning over and into and over,
the way vinyl used to when it got scratched.

Actaeon, Closing Arguments

In art the story varies. An antique vase
has Artemis firing the coup de grace
at Actaeon, still man, devoured.
In later works, when myth was sure
as memory, the hounds are heard to howl
for their lost master whom they've killed
unknown. What draws us into the cave
of the tale is our strong step
toward weakness—the splash
giggling into a mix of porcelain chimes
whose origins no male could help but hunt.
And then, ambushed by the gold of unfired thighs
divinely sunk in a human bath, the straying
marksman must have felt the brink
that danger pushes onto lust to make it fine.
The goddess' character witnesses,
nymphs et al, assure it was
his silence she procured
when his virility was torn
into antler and hide. The hounds, alas,
loyal first to what they know themselves
to be, met the master's snorted pleas
with their jaws. The artists over time
have grown ambiguous moral in their telling.
For some, the instant's shame reminds us
sin hunts in packs swaggering home,
red muzzled and eyes kindled.
Yet, strangely, it is the shuddered flanks
of her girls pearled in spring who never break
from their multitude to hide their master,
that captures the scene in Titian and Galloche.
Artemis alone knows her dogs well.

At the Chest of Drawers (1936)

after the painting by Stanley Spencer

Alone we can lose anything, but it takes company
to find it again. The woman holds on to the upper
drawer with her right hand, reaching with her left

into the bottom drawer which the man pulls out.
She stands on her left leg, the right swung
out from the iris-storm print of her dress.

Something lurks within the pages of their bed,
a bag, an umbrella, a sheathed blade. It clubs
out its side like a head to curiously watch

their search of the chest. Licks of fabric erupt
from the open top drawer which she ignores,
and at bottom two clumps of garment eyeball

her frantic ballet. He is shadow. He is always
the foil, brown and difficult, squat-flattened,
the stone in the garden path, the rock in the stream.

The sky of the scene is the white labial sheets
above the cagey lined mattress. What they find
is neither thing nor idea. It escapes into both of them.

Lupanar

Sábana Grande, Caracas

Where the wolf is free
to be a man, let shoulders blossom

barely, let slender legs cinnamon
the air. These are velvet entrails

where cushions womb the elbow
of the arm angled, ending on a cigar

poised between fingers like a woman
on a brass bar, dance polished.

One comes upon their flesh
here unafraid. The nymphs do not startle

around a maiden deity stubbornly naked
and armed. No dignity to cure.

The hunter is fellowed by other men,
and all are dogs with no master

to chase in confusing growls
by the music of a spell.

We pay, mount, and tremble.
Wash, dress, dip into our loafers,

hum the night into afterthought.
The stranger no different from the lover.

Like money, mirrors and the grave, sex lies beyond us—
the body's zen for which the night was made.

Cartoneros, Buenos Aires

Corrientes, the street that never slept,
now drapes its nights with rubbish.

Beggars and street dwellers rip
the obsidian trash bags left on the curb

for morning pickup in search
of recyclables—cardboard, plastics—

and bejewel the pavements
with the bags' limp and shiny entrails.   .

Trained in impossible beauties
by years of art fairs and performances

and those damned installations,
I am driven past an urban scene

that merits gallery lights and labels.
Behold I must in vapid places

the mazes of intention. My words
have too much pretended the curling brow,

and sighed as theory rattled the life
of reason it padlocked. So now feast

on the art that is everywhere
in the city I once loved to walk,

laureled by wine and cigar smoke,
where I had met with Borges and knew women

who prompt no calendars in my memory,
and siren yet the streets of joy,

for the pearls I once bit from their necks
and not the glass I crunch beneath my sole

when I step from the cab and dodge
laborious shadows in front of my hotel.

Beggar

". . . the heart recovers quickly from someone else's grief."
—*Pindar,* Nemean Odes, *no. 1, epode 3*

"Keep your arm out and hand up,
as if you were begging," says the new doctor
taking my blood pressure for our first time
together. She scrutinizes me, turns me
like a morsel in the mouth of her mind,
sorting the sodiums and cilantros and temperatures
that wrote the bio of my stumbling
onto her Petri dish, a refugee
from a defunct insurance plan,
startled to detect the newness of my old
conditions, de-comforted, misaligned
with what I no longer needed to confess.
Shirtless in the examining cold,
I slump into a nirvanian mound.
"No exercise of any kind," she confirms,
and I riposte, "I walk five miles a day."
Later she is hurtfully surprised to read
my perfectly normal electrocardiogram.
I who lived in the sways
of an anonymous shore
must now meet the cross
flapping on the banner, follow the steel tip
of the sword coursing the sand.
"Anything else I need to know?" she asks,
and I want to argue that I am not
the sum of dips and jiggles
on a looped sheet my heart walked,
that I am a betrayed husband,
and that the toll of three cigars a day
is nothing compared to that

and the encroaching symmetry
of this year's birthday, 54,
which is also the year I was born
in the past century and she never came back
and begged to be made alien by forgiveness.
The doctor will probably misspell my name
on our first prescription. But she doesn't.
Hyphen and all, everything is
where it should be, even though
I am the last patient of her day.

Solvitur Ambulando

The man used to walk four miles a day,
two hours at first, less as he got stronger
and thinner, to defy the sense of rules that dictates
higher challenges as the ability climbs. Rebel
mind in a rebel body. Not even Plato's
philosopher escaped the cave on logic alone.
He gutted. He fed the incipient. The machine
simply rumbled and smoked, but he refused
to stitch the causal quilt and rather slipped
into light quite unwrappingly, birthday
eyes all full of disbelief. But not belief,
for faith is logic-weaned, owes it the farm
where happening-onto is a stranger,
stranger than a broken plow, stranger than walking
off the great betrayal of the once loved.
Proof: all journeys are circular, emptying and deaf.

Regina

On the approaches to her 100th birthday,
the long stretch of peasant light
that guided her from Asturias to Havana
to Chicago to Miami
split into a hundred cackles of delight,
as mariachis on the 5 p.m. talk show
turned to her to wave and flirt
and beg her to let them play a song for her,
any song, *Cielito Lindo* or *El Rey*,
and she waved back and said, No No,
I won't let you in, though let me think about
the one with the big-bellied guitar, No No,
not even him, not today, O my that they should
want an old woman like me, No No I won't
give you the key to the house.

You'll just have to sing from out there,
from the tamarind streets of my youth
where my light used to hum
past the lace of carnations
entwined in clouds of cigar
along columned porches by the sea,
and is walking dancing so sprightly now,
yes yes, so sprightly,
and will never return to me.

Cuba, Where Art Thou?

What if it were not
such a tragedy
to outlive
one's nation,
if it were simply
an invitation
to accept all doors
to all hallways, however
dark and cold, as gates
of the amphitheater at Pergamum
rising, fanning
impossibly heroically
up the misty flanks,
however steep
and rough, aspiring
to the summit calmed
by the shadow rungs of temple,
forum and library,
and the Great Altar
of Zeus, square and crowning it all,
wreathed in titanic fighters
and screeching gods,
and for many decades now
in Berlin.

Monsters

I confess
nothing drew me
to their comic kind
when my years made natural
their allure. The huge ape
circus-bound yet deeply
in impossible love, scaling,
then falling in a hail,
was neither troubling
nor braced with the lightning rod
destinies of desire.
Nor did the great lizard—
fire-eyed and crater-breath,
calmly venturing across
a livid metropolis
of guns and screams, bridges
failing like cardboard—
entice the scroll of fantasy.
Now, theory-armed
and like a miner
seeking to gem a culture's lows
out from the vulgate dark,
I watch the stammering flicks
and glossy remakes,
roll the plastic toys
in the tide of my grown hands,
and understand America
as a ship run aground in allegory.
Its childhood id was chained
and hauled across the sea,
and tossed among the granite monuments

clutching his blond trinket.
Behold the towering reptile,
the adult id finally breaking
the spell of regimen, not to glow
in the earned zenith, but to burn
in a rage of vices. I know why
their aberrants did not speak
to me, in flight from a breathing monster,
and why I refuse to forsake
the right to renaissance—privately,
if that is how it has to be.

Siege

"A enemigo que huye, puente de plata."
[*For the enemy in flight, a silver bridge."*]
   —Spanish saying, attributed to Gonzalo Fernández
   de Córdoba (1453–1515)

after a view of Havana painted by Ismael Gómez-Peralta

In the painting the city or a part of it,
the part the rain lets you see or the paint
acting like rain and mist, denying
or allowing really this part to come forth
or, dispensing with will, let us just say
distance and the weather conditions
have their say. Or their equivocations.
Their tactics, their thesaurus of intent,
by which the city resumes its walled
desire but, as with modern things
in general, mobile, so the wall is
in actuality the window of the car
in which you are being taken
to a banquet or prison or the airport
as the rain oils its lavish elongated domes
on the pane, feathered by accelerations
the painter registers with elegant spare arcs
and the silver calligraphies of an age in flight.

The Sons-in-Law, Sodom

Genesis 19:14

What makes you think, old man,
a place that rose before my memory
could die in our time?

We've been besieged, and taken once
or twice, yet shook off those histories
to tell of them, and maybe jot

a lesson here and there. We've seen
the desert but never without
our spire's imprint or the shrouding wall.

Look, see the flesh quivering on my arm
and the muscle's curl. Would you dream
men could outrun marble and word?

And if they could, they'd be condemned
to ponder lost belonging from a foreign place.
Who would wish to bury one's only land?

We will stay in the shadows that know us,
made us men and will surely mourn us.
Sodom ends each time we die.

Daytime Moon

It nurses the stubborn lost,
thumbs its only print
on the blue crime scene of the sky.

Driving through the Everglades,
one sees it shape a pallor familiar.
The mottled disk muses anomaly

and makes the point no one can miss—
oddness is the heart's true north,
hoping against all evidence

that each is truly each, that we are not
the harp blurred solid by strum,
the spokes of the loom or the fingers

of a frantic hand. That every passion
and idea disowns the ingredient fate
of solids stewed, and that we hover

island steady in fertile solitude at such times,
misplaced like the whitest moon,
skull the sharpened sun has thinned

upon anodyne sands. Let night
paint her in silver and red, and in lavenders
be she eclipsed. In harvests plated.

Let branches demure her behind anthracite fans.
By day, sprung from her dark net, like us
she becomes a refugee, home burning,

the woman who turned pity into salt.
She is scripture's first and rarest sculpture,
the goddess of art as sinful sacrifice.

Democracy,

Borges said, is a superstition.
If so, it is a dark hope.
No masses rise, no dope
disowns his dopiness.

The gears bite into each other
but do not grind down
to perfect, shiny, round
disks. No garden of mirrors

here. The brunt of beast
is history. Except to say so
is allowed. Idea might go
and fetch the bone of progress

yet. Art's riot, medicine,
the tracked moon, the internet,
all the falling apples bet
on cranky, subtle elevation.

So we read the shells
on crisp statistical maps
and stumble off in laps,
that bent race, that spiral

into future. Not a straight
line in the place, nor steps,
but a drain that treads
the zero freedoms emulate.

Variation on Quevedo's Variation on Seneca, Ovid

Miré los muros de la patria mía

He teaches that a gaze can crumble the walls
that once a country held, and that the storm
of time leaves wells of decrepitude.
Puddles really, but as my father taught me,
You see a patch of water on the road,
and no one knows what's in it,
so drive around it. The jaws of depth lurk.
Dip your tires like bread and it may be
your last supper. I drove over the hole
to test his theory, for its oily bronze
made my eye feel it was a minor
hold. The car shook and sure enough
he came back with his Spanish aphorism—
The devil knows more because he is old,
than because he's the devil. I would,
like Quevedo, vanish into fields
where there are no walls and the paths
are not betrayed by their bucklings.
The road of exile has no markings.
Shot at six along the beam that still hurtles
from a star consigned to was,
and will be, and now brittling,
I am the backpack and the bitterness,
quartermaster and siren. I will tell
what I know to those who know it.
The rest drive round the placid shimmers
sure the road not tested is good as gold.

Artemisa Japanese Car Care, Miami

I step out of the shop where my old car
gets younger, and see as if for the first time
the triangular communications tower
looming to the south. My father, the draftsman,
would have glanced at the structure, tapering,
branched on each side by lined arrays of equipment,
and calculated strengths and forgeries,
named and numbered steels
that for my aesthetic eye are burnished metals
in a skeletal bauhaus with minimalist flashes.

The gulfs never quarreled between us.
To each man, assigned domains bestow
province and legion, a shield of bridge
across the darkness blows.
A wisdom hails from what is not,
to the other, strange. I imagine my father
torpor-free on such a tower's ways.
The sky celluloid it takes for ladders,
the host-cream drums with which a million
chatters moon and back—he'd raise
such gallows up from plans he drew
in ballet surgeries, the way a sterile God
first dreamed snow, and in a leap
planted it in our denials.

His muse did not know recoil
between the draftsman's cage
and the welder's theater, which let him
bin with pride over my poems and scrape
to buy paintings he understood

without understanding. And how he must
have hoped and dared to prophesy
this moment, at this car mechanic's,
when I at centuries last see him
in all the labors of Velázquez's Forge.
The swagger of grime Praxiteles
receiving delicate news from a robed gardenia,
arc the prism of identity, thinkers to tamers.
But in my father alone have I witnessed
a brotherhood in one self, a forum
made for them within one man.
Nineteen years after your death,
your slow son,
who natured only to beauty and ideas,
has come home.

The Prodigal's Brother

He was the shadow that held
the father up when,
sweeping the swept-clean
horizon with his eyes,
the old man sighed off
another good night.

A darkness numb
spoke itself between
the dutiful axle of son
and the patient wheel
of the father, a millstone
in a landscape, a season
punctual, a wedding
that follows all the rituals.
How unlike art

life was. He had nurtured
hopes for the stage,
a life of images and paint,
the tossed rhyme
which nonetheless
captures an age. He left
that for future men

to teach with stories,
live their lives into a poem,
perish in martyrdom's
ardent reviews. A fancy dinner,
or was it a simple repast
for brutes who would change

the world? He could hear
the neighing of the wooden planks
being rolled into his world.

He imagined destiny
coming army bright
and clanging, and he tended
the laborious sheep and field,
pruned the vine,
and swore the rightness
that flowed from it
would never
abandon him.

That's when the story
asked him to stand there.
No, over there. The young
tattered whose choices
removed him from the nature
of this fold
had returned, and the joy—
as if defeat and mercy
could, mating, undo
what the broken had
willingly become—
struck his brow
thorned with injustice.

Finally, it wasn't
happiness or its lightning
that got to him,

but, dutifully—
when everyone else
was snoring feast into tale—
how he had to drag that shovel
up the rocky hill
that had waited for him,
and bury
forgiveness
now that it too had squandered
its place
in the golden day.

Little Ones

Matthew 19:14

Bring them, the little ones,
for those like them will inherit the kingdom,
cottony sighted, wooly edged,
bumbling onto this then that, unchecked
by focus, reason, or remorse. They hoard
and delight in the other's need,
and when the weaker one cries
it is an anthem that confirms
their strength. Bring them, for they
are the models of the wondrous heart.
They pin the lizard to the anthill,
cast the fleeing moth into the web,
hurl stones at the scurrilous cat.
They search through an empty lot
to find glass and rust, plastic and coil
and turn them into treasure
or the enchanted prism or the kingly
medal or the certain sign. Who make
of worn belts snakes, swords of broomsticks,
wizardries of bent coins, they
will crown themselves on the only day
that matters. They who howl
and revel in dirt and piss. They
who tribe into pounding fists
and rob the hunted one
of all prayer. Bring them.
Be them. For in a fury
of obeisance denied, did not I
cast waves upon the earth
and rains thicker than falling gold?
Angry I was not obeyed, did not I

curse the tree that withheld or gave too much?
Did I not gift unevenly lights
to all my children, that some should be lost
in bestowed darkness while others
be set in the porcelain ways?
Bring them, for I shall make them see
the blood in their games as mine.

Lamb

after the painting Zanimo *(Animal) by Ernst Prophète*

Otherwise, the pink
sky would denote
tenderness, a girl
fumbling through
her mother's rouge.
But here a lamb trembles
knee-deep in a blue stream
watched by a wolf on the bank.

The earth, the sky are beaten red.
Calm plants punctuate,
wreathe the scene.
As if the slaughter
that must come
heralds accomplishment.

Is that the only amulet
against lamentation?
In truth, the wolf
has come late to the hope
of killing, for the lamb
in his blue gullet
has already been devoured
by time, as have been
the dry wolf and the merciful,
marching trees.